FINISHING LINE PRESS
www.finishinglinepress.com

The Only One in the Room with White Socks

poems by

Michael Northen

Finishing Line Press
Georgetown, Kentucky

The Only One in the Room with White Socks

ISBN 979-8-89990-512-4 First Edition

Publisher: Leah Huete de Maines

Editor: Christen Kincaid

Cover Art and Design: Elijah Northen.

Author Photo: Michael Northen

Order online: www.finishinglinepress.com
also available on amazon.com

Author inquiries and mail orders:
Finishing Line Press
PO Box 1626
Georgetown, Kentucky 40324
USA

Contents

Dedication or quote

Mom: San Francisco, 1943

She's wearing glossy black high heels
strapped around the ankles, the shine
of the evening sun reflecting off her nylons.
There is nothing of the farm girl in her.
The dark coat cuts just at the knee
fur-lined collar open to reveal
a hint of the white-pleated skirt beneath.
Wherever she's going, it isn't to milk cows.
Buildings of the city rise in the background
behind the triangle of park where she's posed.
The word that describes this day is beyond her reach:
Halcyon.
I'm grateful that she doesn't see
the truck that's on its way to haul her home
to a despotic father,
(this young new wife whose husband is at sea)
or the seven children and seventy years
that stretch out ahead of her like a savannah
without a nightclub in sight.

Belts

In another photo,
my younger brother is wearing suspenders
while I have a belt, a sign that I'm
responsible enough to care for myself.
Our shirts tucked in,
neat and clean was the motto
of those who could not change their clothes every day.

Yesterday my belt broke, the buckle
snapping clear of its leather strap,
a manifest metaphor
of our increasing obsolescence.
Today it is all sweat pants and pajama bottoms
and even jeans with belt loops
are designed to ride low on the ass,
quite a sight for old folks on porches
who remember
when hand-me-downs were not a choice
and ripped jeans were not
 worn with insouciance
by those who trudged into the fields
at first light.

Ulcer

The ulcer on my mother's ankle
radiated outward in violet, magenta
and pink rings to golf ball size,
the middle a small caldera that issued forth
its clear, syrupy liquid.
At times it lay dormant but when bumped
bloomed again like a malignant rose.

She delighted in waving it around
watching the discomfort on our faces
as she gave the morning ulcer report.
Some days each of us seven children
were met with a performance as we rose
and walked to breakfast in the kitchen.

As a teenager, I was a good boy
keeping my room clean, saying my prayers
showing deference to elders,
and trying to fill my absent father's shoes.
I was never willful.
But when she would greet me in the morning
(oatmeal already on the table)
waving that throbbing canker in the air
like a jester performing for a Tudor court
I would not give what she was asking for:
compassion.

Madison Pub

Ed and I shake the water from our hats
as record rain follows us through the restaurant door.
We hang Mom's jacket and cane on a coat hook
and hoist her to the bar stool
at a table in the Madison Pub,
our ark against these times.
Two Yuengling drafts and a hot tea fortify us
and for a while the water drowns
the iniquities in Iraq, the genocide in Sudan
the sexual prejudice in our own land
as through the window we watch the deluge descend
over the track of the train that brought us here.

Ed and I talk of smaller things:
his last shift fighting fires
my work with disabilities
the distance between California and the east,
thatching together our thoughts after so many years.
Mom looks on, the half-blind, half-deaf prophet
with a French dip sandwich
repeating between bites the same old tales
as though each time they were new.

As we step out the rain still falls as obstinately
as bullets and body parts fall over Baghdad
but in the water our feet touch ground
and somewhere in the wind, we hear a raven's caw
and smell the scent of olive leaves
blowing in from Ararat.

Erasure Poem: Two Ships

I.
My parents are like two ships in a harbor,
A tired simile but like my parents it still serves.
My mother is white with painted palm trees and flags flying
A cruise ship—clean, built well, open to all
A friendly stewardess waves to you from the deck
As you board humming old show tunes.
You know you will have a great time.
Small, serviceably gray, my father is the ship you pass by.
He has seen the Aleutian mists, Pearl Harbor being bombed
Skirted rainy Korean war, felt green in New Caledonia sun.
He will not say which port is best.
And there is one thing more.
My mother is the ship that never leaves the harbor.
My father is the ship that never returns.

II.
My parents two ships
my parents still .
My mother is white
clean open to all
friendly waves to you from the deck
humming old show tunes.

my father you pass by.
He has seen Aleutian mists, Pearl harbor
Korean war, New Caledonia sun.
which is best.

My mother never leaves the harbor.
My father never returns.

III.

parents
still
mother white

humming

father you pass by

war
is best

never

Plan of Care: The Nurses Say She Rambles

When the flood came we had to move to the attic.
We lost all the chickens.
I don't want to go back to that home.
Dad was on the USS Rochester when Judi was born.
In El Sobrante, Beakins came late.
They were drunk and stole all our furniture.
The Navy was supposed to move us.
Dad went out on the USS Rochester.
The nurses said they were going to tie me in a bag and throw me
 in a river.
I'm so tired.
We moved from South Dakota for Grandpa's health.
He got the arthritis and sold the farm.
The potato soup was good today.
You have to go home on Friday don't you?
I don't want to go back to that home. Nobody talks.
When the flood came Grandpa said, "Watch the Filipinos.
They'll steal the chickens."
We went to Reno to get married because they were shipping Dad out
On the USS Rochester.
I loved that job in San Francisco at Nabisco.
But Grandpa and Uncle John came up and moved me back home.
I don't know if I had another stroke.
What did you say?
I'm not going to take 20 pills.
When we came out from South Dakota I had to go work for Uncle Ray
To pay him back.
We lost everything in the flood.
At that home they were putting medicine in my food.
What's a UTI?
Dave, when Ed was born and I had the blood clot.
I'm sorry you had to go live with Uncle Harry.
I didn't want to sell my home. I didn't want to sell my home.
I'd just finished talking to Mike on the phone and I had
Spaghetti on the stove. I don't know what happened.
What did you say?
I've been cooperating. I didn't do anything.
I don't want to go back to that home.

I like the food here.
I've got a good memory.
That apartment was at 1739 Pine St. in San Francisco.
Grandpa wanted boys but he got six girls first.
Do you remember when we lived in the Quonset huts?
What did you say?
I'm tired.
I *do* cooperate.

Second Drowning

This was not like the time before when I almost drowned
when the water lay above like a thick ceiling I could not reach.
Then I saw the sunlight diffuse through the water
leaning back in that golden acceptance, I closed my eyes.

This time it was like a Japanese painting.
The anesthesiologist said, count to three.
I was only a plum branch sketch on canvas
white disappearing into white.

The problem was only mechanical I told my mother
through a phone in her nursing home room
a valve in the heart that needed repair.
I'd tell you to come home, she said, but I don't have one.

This time it was whiteness. No gold water calling.
"Our Father" my mother said, as she fingered the beads,
her prayers traveling in a circle. We knelt on the floor.
Our fingers circulating again through the old design.

Little Litany

"If you understand anything about God, he is not in it."
—Meister Eckhart

She is not among the pixels in the picture on my computer desktop.
She is not in the breeze blowing among the gladiolas in the yard that is no longer hers.
She is not in the memory-carrying synapses firing from nerve to nerve.
She is not even in the casket overlooking the desert park at the edge of the cemetery.
She is not in the printed words of her obituary.
She is not in the frozen soil of South Dakota or the rays of a careless California sun.
She is not anywhere to be found among the coconut and peanut butter chips of her magic bars
And even though I listen carefully, she is not in the lyrics of "Springtime in the Rockies"
Or in a silent coda of the *ite misa est.*
She is not.

Crocuses

The first day of February crocuses
are coming up through the colorless lawn
their thin violet petals like the skirts of angels.
I think of my mother, singing in heaven.
She has joined the choir and is chatting with Gabriel and Michael
distracting them from their daily hymns.
The arthritis is gone from her fingers,
the cataracts cleared from her eyes
and she moves with the guileless grace she had as a girl.
It's the reward that belief has prepared her for
after a life of disappointment and constant toil,
watching now for those children who'll follow her,
though not all of us will.

Last week my wife and I picked out our burial sites,
a hillside overlooking the river in a troubled city.
The only angels greeting us will be stone
vying for space with gargoyles that guard
the gravestones and mini-mausoleums.
Our grandchildren will come and picnic,
throwing Frisbees and drinking hefeweizen,
smiling with forbearance at our dreams of world peace,
crocuses that sprang from an indifferent soil.

March 21

First day of spring,
beneath the residue of last year's leaves
the ghosts of November plants are stirring
their colorless first shoots
quickening into life.

Not everything that dies returns again:
the pansies, catchfly, marigolds
or my brother gone 50 years
and absent on this birthday
sealed in a past untouched by spring.

He lives solely in our minds
those engines that can pull time
only down a one way track
disappearing further each spring
in the rearview mirror.

To be human means to be forgotten,
the way the soil will soon forget
the new life it cradles this year:
the pansies, catchfly, marigolds
and all earth's psalms that make
our brief lives beautiful.

April

The irises are too late for Easter.
They have taken a different path
bodying out in new guise
from small, shrunken tubers
to a world still chlorophyll and carbon
sunlight and soil
no remembrance of self, if self
or remembrance were possible.

What are we to do
now that Saturday is past
and it's still raining
but look for recognition
in the bend of an earthworm
or some hint of memory
in a sudden shift or air.
Droplets shining on the leaves
are not grace
but dew condensing to remind us
that all is evaporation and return.

Good Friday

When my sister died I planted an azalea
in the backyard here in the east
at the interstice of spring and winter.
But her ashes were given to the wind
out among the Joshua trees.
This past year preta have roamed the land,
hungry ghosts driven by their own despair
swept in from the desert on the Santa Anas
seeking to consume, divide, destroy.
The tips of the azalea splay out in threes
an inert brown, like crosses on a hill.
April has not touched them yet,
but they are late bloomers.
It takes more warmth than this
for the sap to rise again.

Confiteor

In the Act of Contrition, I would say
I was sorry for my sins
"because I dread the loss of heaven
and the pains of hell."
Later that was changed to
"because of thy just punishment."
At times I'm glad I no longer believe in God
as when my sister died last spring,
an alcoholic who abandoned her children
and stole from everyone who helped her.
I don't know what her just punishment would be
but I'm sure the Mojave where we
scattered her ashes is kinder.
And I think Dante would approve.
Nothing there can coax care
from the sun-scared stones
and any acts of contrition the wind carries
are reduced to exactly
what our lives have been worth.

Nicotiana

Pulling crabgrass from the nicotiana
July sun shining through the cloud cover
like a convection oven

In the street men in hard hats and yellow vests
tear the asphalt, machine scraping
down to the cobbled road beneath
grueling work but at least they are well paid
unlike those who worked under the same sun
pulling tobacco in Richmond County
while the Constitution was being signed
tethered to land that my family owned for 200 years

Air wavers with the heat
the sweat on my face drips with a taste like privilege
watering the flowers below
on a day when sky is the color of smoke
from the Pall Malls my father inhaled
until the day he died.

Homestead

The old homestead would have been
Half a mile from the river between the two swamps
But even in 1900 when my grandfather was a boy
Observers wrote, "it is in a very sad state of repair."
When first built on a patent from the British crown
It looked across tobacco fields, housed eighteen kids
One of whom died in the Revolutionary War
And down the river a still, rum for colonial troops.
But William's will said he had slaves
And his son
And his son…
Perhaps even some who bore his name.
So, good, you say
Good.
Let the wilderness take back what wickedness wrought.
I could agree, if only
The pants I'm wearing did not come from
A sweatshop in Malaysia
And my Nikes weren't made with child labor
Or I hadn't just heard the waitress
Who served up the bargain burger I just bought
Say that her heat may be turned off again.
Privilege always parks its chair
On the misery of others.
I only follow this map to unearth it
Acknowledge it
And carry on.

Rappahannock

Rappahannock flows through fields
Like time
Around lives
Like Coltrane
Riffing on the past
Around the tobacco farm in Farnham
Roof rotted
The wooden graves gone, gone
And it flows around a memory
Of a grandmother's body
Weighed down with stones…
Above the dry fields of Aberdeen
It becomes wind
The steady bass beat of hammer on hard ground
Summer dust bowl
Blowing families out to California
Moving outward to the tonic
Looking for that home key
Was there ever one?
Jazz is not return
The Rappahannock is not return
The wind is not return
Only a rhythmic sprawl
Unable to renounce its past
Growing, morphing, changing register

Collingswood Park

listless
the air bathwater calm
a plane overhead escapes this mirage
leaving its hum in the placid blue
my eyes slipping closed
head resting on a picnic table
teenagers in the swings seem
as far away as childhood
a calm zephyr carries this life away
maple leaves in plainchant
the afternoon a fable
about to dissolve

Maggie in the pool

not a fish exactly but a naiad
whose body seeks
the sea,
an affinity evading logic.
When asked what she likes about the water
she says, "Everything."
No wonder the whirr of written words and rules
elude her,
the way it separates the world
from self.
Who wouldn't want to dip
into the Aegean on a shore before time
raising a conch shell to their ear
as Aphrodite rises from the waves?

Letter from Dubai

I sit in a mirage:
Tall buildings of glass and steel
rising out of a stony desert
inhabited only by ghosts of the future.
Sparrows prattle from the palms
and warm breezes full of the scent of sea
blown in by some jinn.
I must be in the California of my childhood,
the sky Disney blue.
The seed pods have been stripped from the acacia trees
only one still holds them—too high for me to reach.
Doves bobbing their speckled necks coo softly
something in Arabic I think
modulated in monosyllables like the call to prayer.

For Jackson

Along the edge of the Delaware
you build a play house of algae
and driftwood you've found
strung like scoured bones
just beyond the water line,
a home that could shelter only
an imagination like yours.
We're always constructing something,
even ourselves,
out of what the current carries.
I see you at two in a red dress with daisies
and now, eschewing all but what a boy would wear.
When I was young I lived in naval housing
and houses of stucco all built from fixed design
that always made me wonder where I belonged.
I prefer your algae house
the way it is open to the sun
and lets new breezes pass through.
It won't be afraid to change
when the river knocks it down.

Messenger

Heat pushing 100 degrees
my head no place for poetry
at the edge of Cooper River
I sit on a log
below the silver maples.
Sunlight on the round quartz stones
beneath the water
gilds them like Byzantine madonnas.

In the distance
geese appearing on the lazy current
begin to stir as I sit.
First gathering
then closing ranks like a flotilla
they swim forward, some turning in profile
others stretching their necks towards me.
The leader thrusts his head forward
and stares.

I watch until he turns silently
and they retreat into the river
dissolving into warm ripples
against the other shore.
Their silence limns the water
a minnow skims the stones
at the water's edge
where varicolored leaves clump
with the feathers and empty plastic bottles
at my feet.

Opossum

He was stuck in the trap
set for our lettuce marauder,
bottom jaw wedged in the metal frame
he'd tried to chew through,
curved teeth hooked in
and cinched around the wire.
Blood pooled beneath,
a blank reptilian stare betraying
the Mesozoic refugee he was.
I grabbed the jaw and clubbed, turned,
clubbed it with my hand
until the face popped loose.
Stunned for a moment
he sat, not even seeing me
then turned and waddled
into the undergrowth from which he'd come
as though civilization had never existed.

Trouble Brewing

is the name of the coffee shop
where I'm sitting in suburban NJ.
Fans swirl from the ceiling
and people around us chatter
eating grilled cheese sandwiches and
working on their computers.
I'm writing in my notebook
as I did midnight 40 years ago
at Truckadero in Indio,
hair to my shoulders and baby Maya
beside me in her chair on the table
desert wind humming outside.
Trouble is brewing
as Israeli soldiers prepare to savage Gaza
razing homes, schools and hospitals,
leaving children lying like litter in the streets,
all in the name of revenge.
It's a different kind of desert
one where winds of hate obscure
moral responsibility.
I sip the coffee uneasily:
my baby is still alive

First Day of Winter

after Jane Kenyon

Orange has fled the marigolds.
Sparrows search the remains of sunflower heads.
Fresh bread fills the kitchen

and on the stove soup bubbles
from the last of the turkey bones.
Let winter come.

Ribbons and wrapping paper put away.
What can be wrapped is wrapped.
What can be tied is tied.

After fall's final flourish
What is there left to do
but let winter come?

All is in readiness.
Our heavy coats hang in the hall.
The cane leans by the door.

The husks that rattle in the furrows now
were resting in the corn we sowed in spring.
Let winter come.

Et Tu

No snow this winter.
Between the frost and thaw
I scoop ashes from the summer's barbecue
and toss them into the bare ground
that will be garden in spring.
Scoop upon scoop of
black flakes scatter, lending the soil
the look of ground in a war torn country
say, Ukraine
where there will be no growing this year.

We're appalled, of course
watching images of destruction
the buildings in ruin
the faces of the children killed
paraded across the TV screen
and wonder how anyone could justify
such hatred
or stand by and watch it happen.

How it could happen
that people are shot in churches and grocery stores
that schools search students for weapons
that teachers are told to arm themselves
that guns are more available than healthcare?

Rich in calcium, potassium, magnesium
ashes are good for growing tomatoes.
In the coming season
we should have a bumper crop.

Epidemic

We've survived the winter cold.
At an outdoor café, masks have lifted.
Sparrows pick at the food dropped
beneath the table by toddlers.
Mower hums in the distance.
I pour over family history notes.

According to their headstones
the brothers died a month apart
in the "Year of the Schoolhouse Blizzard"
before South Dakota became a state.
Having come from the Alps to
homestead the recalcitrant land
they survived the snow.
But a colder something killed them:
an unseen mystery in the air
that swelled tongues and choked off breath
in days before anyone knew
what bacteria was or could name it.

There's an empty table next to me
warm in the sunlight
a circle of dandelions
that winter has not mown down.
I imagine it is reserved for the children
of those who claimed to love them
those who had the knowledge
who could have worn a mask
but wouldn't.

At a Café Montreal

Trying to force her way among the café tables
the rotund tourist whacks a pitcher
with her bag
sending the water into my salad where it floats
like algae on a tidal reef
before pouring onto my pants.
Blessed with a warm autumn day in Montreal,
its hard not to laugh as the waitress races
to the table with towels.
We could be in Florida instead where a
hurricane has left thirty people dead
and no amount of towels will clean up the mess.

How have we come to the place
where the only time we help each other
is after the storm has hit
and the damage done?
This café isn't large but
there is space at all the tables
if each customer is willing to
give up a little instead of
plunging ahead like a bullish traveler
eyes only on their own needs.

The Dead Come

The dead come to us demanding an explanation.
They show us the cracks in their hands, their pock-mocked faces.
They carry in threadbare shawls the babies that died in birth.
They ask through teeth worn bare by chewing grain or gristle
how we dare with our soft hands and filigreed words to excoriate their lives,
condemn the way they spoke, the language that they used
why we think we can see the world from the empyrean as God does
past, present, future all condensed into a hazelnut.
Get in line behind us, they say, you'll need our help
when your grandchildren come with their word lists and erasers
reigning ozymandian judgment on your lives.

The Only One in the Room with White Socks

At Corona del Mar surfers with peroxide hair
hauled boards from their woodies
and tossed towels onto the sand
throwing off tennis shoes and white socks
to paddle out and catch a wave.
I wasn't one of the cool kids but
could always spot an east coast tourist,
black socks stretching up pallid legs
from shiny black shoes or bulky sandals
that even on the beach said "up tight."
It fed my adolescent ego, a smugness
born of wanting to belong.

At the writers conference in Philadelphia
hair tending gray, I'm watching youthful fingers fly
over cell phones, brandishing the books they've published
and chanting mantras of social justice.
They're riding a wave I've been caught short of
trying to body-surf.
Knocked under, spinning for direction
I don't understand how life's undertow
has rescinded everything I thought I understood.
I watch it ripple back through all these beautiful bodies.

I'm the only one in the room with white socks.

Babel

I know the confusion the builders felt when the tower fell.
Believing unity was better than discord,
they were only trying to find some stairway to understanding.
It's easy to picture the massive rocks falling
men and women tumbling to their death
crushed beneath the weight of their collective hopes
as an angry god said I will twist your tongues into different languages
so that your words become a scattering of useless sounds.
I will plant the seeds of suspicion
so you believe that everything the others say
is a fable, a noose, or a lie.

No wonder the air is heating up
in this summer of fire and tornados
when global warming is still called a myth
and any attempt to build a structure that
might bind us all together
is labeled a desecration.

We could sit down and talk
tell each other our stories in good faith.
But, of course, you won't believe me
an old middle class man
still white,
still walking
still the gender named by my doctors
at birth.

City

"I returned to the city to feast with death."
—Bob Herz

Halfway across the Ben Franklin I pause,
buildings in shade beneath the covid sky
a single ferry on the river below.
This isn't Augustine's city.

In the absence of normality
something has leaked up from the ground
like a punctured canister of WWI gas
releasing its death into the air.

Car jackings, road rage, the easy gun,
gang shootings in mid-afternoon
the daily dead pile up.
No common dream to be deferred.

Halfway across the Ben Franklin I pause
No vision—only a memory
of peace signs on the boulevard
neighborhood marches to integrate schools
hands linked in solidarity of purpose.

The city glowers ahead.
I will bring no heifer to feast on,
enough throats already slit
enough drinking of blood.

I'm frozen at mid-span
the river waits on either side
as though time were something other
than the mind of man.
This is not a future I will walk into.

The Day Before I Died

After the night rain, blue crept out
from the edges of the spiderwort.

In the street, county workers were mixing asphalt
to repair the cracks left by winter.

We walked into the village along the bike path
that had once been a railroad track

and at the station café sitting out in the sun
inhaled our first coffee of the season like a tonic.

On a bench across from us a school girl strummed
a Joni Mitchell song on her guitar

as the morning bus rattled by
and we checked the date of our grandson's graduation.

You watched the owner of a boutique post signs
for the first sale of the season.

I looked for Fibonacci numbers in the grass.

Abecedarian

All bets were off when I was born.
Breach, pulled out with forceps in
Coronado Hospital. It was not the
delivery my mother expected,
even protesting I could not be her baby
face dark, hair black and matted.
God must have been laughing:
How unprepared she must have felt.
It was quite a beginning.
Jammed in my dresser drawer crib,
knowing nothing
like the proverbial tabula rasa,
mind a blank slate, I had
no thoughts or anticipations
of what I might become.
Perhaps there were
random, unrecognized images
sensations abuzz in my mind.

Time returns me to that state now
unable to recall words, memories only
vestiges of days and locations,
weathering my life into a
xeriscape of
yesterdays forgotten, today counting down to tomorrow's
zero

Archaeology

Digging in the backyard I come across a cache
of old bottles, medicine and beer mostly, cracked
and packed in a confetti of broken glass.
Etched into the brown, green and pale blue arcs
the half names of apothecaries and breweries
silenced by prohibition remain.
Their antiquated terms (dioxygen, tonsiline, almond cream)
language of the past
repeat themselves to me like the words
of the poets I've been excavating, restoring from the past
marginalized writers whose attempts to name themselves
borrowed the language available to them
words as outmoded as *handicapped* and *dumb*
now shoveled over by contemporary piety.
Like me, they did what they could within their understanding.
When I've pulled them from the dirt and cleaned them off
I'll display the bottles, honor the poems
knowing even now the censorial eyes
through which the future will see me.

Seconds

(After Sherwood Anderson)

After apple picking
when the Cortlands, Northern Spies and Romes
are waxed and packed for selling in the stores
and Granny Smiths become applesauce
and Greenings are gone to pie
those who know return to the orchard
to the small, misshapen fruit rejected by the pickers
and finger those bulges in the flesh
where all the juice gathers
then fill their pockets with these apples
and sink their teeth in until all
that pent up sweetness oozes down their chins
redeeming the old fear that whatever is forbidden,
marginalized or thrown away is most delicious.

Donut Day at Inglis House

Fridays the wheelchairs roll in
steered by hand, head, and tongue
in more variety than the donuts they seek
after a week of healthy food.
Coffee is held to the lips and sipped
or drunk through straws,
thickened to the consistency of sap.
Donuts cut into bite size
and forked into mouths,
the pot tilted until the last drop is gone
and chairs power up.
Each donut-eater heads for the door—
jelly, chocolate, sugar, glazed—
every face etched with its own flavor.

Math Instructor

He wheels in using his one good hand
propelling with his working foot
two days growth of nettle on his face
sweat pants halfway down his bare right thigh.
His face holds no sign of charity.
Croaking algabrese he writes equations
demanding answers a second time
when half-deaf he does not hear
their shy first half-replies.
Only their own wheelchairs
keep the class from bolting
this cave of senseless deciduations.
Light from behind shines
on the dry erase board
as his raw voice beats their silence.
is it only *he* that sees
in his crabbed writing,
euclidean elegance?
How can they miss it
the only gift he has to give them
a glimpse at the eternal beauty of form?

MS

it's like
well, it's like
it's like sea lilies in the ocean
bending wherever the current pulls them
it's like people disappearing
in and out of the fog
only its words that vanish
and reappear without connection
and you say that's what i said
and they say no it isn't
it's like sea lilies
it's like words disappearing
it's like in a dream when your hands
get so heavy you can't lift them
and you can't feel them
so they flop like dead fish
and you're afraid
but you know it's a dream
so you scream to wake yourself up
and it's like dead fish flopping
so you scream to wake up

only you don't

Morning Has Broken

Whose room is this? Mine. but not mine
What time
I can't be late for breakfast.

Ringing. ringing. What is it? Where?
The phone. where is it where is it whereisit
Stop ringing. How do I?
Stop ringing. Stop ringing.
The pillow. there.
Is it time for breakfast?
I can't be late.

My son, my daughter and the other one
The one that's not the first one
Why don't they come?
Why don't they call?

My window
grass green outside.
and roses
must be spring
And the birds.
Black birds with red wings.
What are they called.
I lost the word.

Dan Simpson, Reading

Water laps at the edge of Cooper River,
sun just warm enough to compromise
the breeze coming off the water.
Rain-blanched leaves, broken bits of glass,
twigs stripped of bark, splayed feathers—
winter's final graffiti—rim the banks,
notes-in-a-bottle assuring us
that warmth is not far off.

Dan stands behind the podium
fingers skimming Braille letters
as though to unlock the poetry held there
or perhaps it's an organ from which
his own song rises transformed into words.
At the first clap of hands he cautions:
No applause until the end.
He is taking us down a different river
through bends and cadences he knows well,
our noise like gunfire on the bank
jolts us from the journey.
His voice flowing, honest
opens into expanses of coneflower and larkspur,
not our homeland, but familiar.
It's where we've all collaged our memories from
a childhood prank, a father's words,
a glimpse of heaven.
Dan retrieves the bottle bobbing beside us,
deciphering its hexagrams.
His forecast reads:
The yellow sun shines lemonade
which means the sky must be blue.

Cento: Lessening Light

I live in the length of light's long eclipse
now everything falls to me shadows,
mystery and confusion, and now I wonder.
Every night I dream my future
and local musicians play waltzes in a coffee bar,
six different songs—one after another.
I've never been captured by the dark,
I know vulnerability is related to hope:
I'm no stranger to the blues, babe.

Lines:

1. Desmond Kenny, "My Sense of Blind," *My Sense of Blind*, p. 51.
2. Stephen Kuusisto, "Only Bread, Only Light," *Only Bread Only Light*, p. 22.
3. David Simpson, "Why I Never Married," *The Way Love Comes to Me*, p. 11.
4. Jill Khoury, "Disorder, Not Otherwise Specified," *Borrowed Bodies*, p. 19.
5. Stephen Kuusisto, "Letter to Borges from Tampere, Finland," *Letters to Borges* p. 49.
6. Emily Michael, "Encore," *Neotony*, p. 13.
7. Kathi Wolfe, " After Hurricane Sandy," *The Uppity Blind Girl Poems*, p. 23.
8. Daniel Simpson, "A Few Things," *School for the Blind*, p. 29.
9. Constance Merritt, "Gone Courtin' Blues," *Blind Girl Grunt*, p. 39.

Crip Time: Palmyra Cove

At the marsh's edge time slows
like sap in the surrounding rushes,
the water slowly thickening
its flow delayed,
the hedged flow of synaptic signals
from neuron to neuron, from brain to skin.
Crip time.
Lost in the play of sun,
cordgrass and wind-trampled weeds
it's hard to retrieve that narrative
of destination,
hard to corral
the wild fluctuations of space and time
into a vector.
But what's the choice?
Not as easy as cropping the first person singular
and cutting the stops.
Not as simple as saying
"Nowhere to go.
No ego in this poem."

Cento for David Simpson

If I could see, would I have known that this winter
the cries of the crows rained down on me?
If I could see, would I have known
how to let go of myself to gravity?

A tree in some distant woods,
low ecstatic birds singing
of going farther deeper
to the final cadence.
I didn't plan this
And yet I long for the purer music.

There's no room to explain.
Another breeze touches my neck
gentle tremolos with which I harmonize.
Just that simple, that quiet
whole new worlds open
into the future's songs, and why not?

Stuart in Heaven

His wheelchair falls away as he ascends
The hands uncurl that have been curled since birth
His body straightens
With Demosthenes, he spits the pebbles from his mouth
And words come: poetry.
No longer different
He strides the clouds like Herakles
Glowing in God's justice.

At first the streets seem bare
But then he sees them rolling through the gilded streets
The angels, all in chairs approaching
Like the mute invasion of a motorcycle town
And he, now Gulliver, hears the laugh
Of a desert wind gone mad,
God wild-eyed on a gurney,
Drooling

Schrödinger's Cat Again

for Denise March

I was thinking of you yesterday.
How you could not keep serious
and would wheel into the classroom
with your corny jokes.
Your poems more like Erma Bombeck
than Robert Frost,
stories of your adoption and
your mother insisting to schools that you could learn.
How we'd both lived in Orange County in those days
far from Philadelphia.
I know that when I retired, the classes dissolved.
The poetry workshop, too.
But you've kept me up on the news.
I knew I'd always hear from you
when someone else's chair was empty.

Then the message came.

To Larry Eigner

In August the last of the Wordgathering founders died.
Like you, they lived in chairs.
Like you, they wrestled with speech.
Like you, they wrote what they could see
from a porch, a yard, a window
(bird tree sky)
But they wanted their stories in the world
wanted to let others know the work of poets like themselves.

You yourself said,
don't think of yourself
there is always something else

They had no objective poetics
only what experience had taught them
and the hope that others would want to know.
Narration is no sin when it brings
hidden names to life.
And they, too, had names: Stu, Dana, Yvette, Denise.

You would not approve of this poem
but like their work
it honors you.

Bar Routine

chalk-dusted hands grip the bar as she swings & circles vault & beam
below zoom in & out of view the manic rise to the ceiling suddenly
the floor below fast unstoppable *the future flashes how to modulate
the cyclothymic circle how to halt the sudden rush of thoughts breaking
unbidden into speech that explodes the daisy-lined lane to marriage
home happiness how to break the centripetal force without crashing*
from handstand she swings down into the giant her feet clear of the
low bar kick out behind almost arching her body at the bottom of the
swing pulling her feet into the lead she scoops to bring herself back
for the dismount release *release from angry words from modulating
medicines from accusatory half-empty closets from desperate 2 a.m.
calls* she locks arms straight to keep from pulling back into the bar
in layout position she starts the flyaway rotates & tucks airborne she
imagines the possibility of perfect dismount the return of feet to solid
floor not just sticking the landing but nailing it

mycelium

encountering

An

OBJECT

two

hypha tendrils

split fan

tips tendrils out

reaching exploring no without

out body pre-formed

limitation patterns

Blocking

who

can

say

what how

intelligence evolution

is has to

be

Don't try

to be objective

ginkgos against blue sky

two bolts of gingham

rusty lug nut

conceived in liberty and dedicated to the proposition

e = mc2

no ideas [maybe] but in things

escondido I

frag

ment

ed

boom shakka laka

It's always you.

Summa

i'm
turn
ing
back
to form

from
the freed
words
and dis
continuities
wrested from
rhyme & rhythm
what I shook off in youth
breaking those patterns
that held us in place

Give me a child until seven Augustine said
and he's mine for life. The child is returning.

Leaves descend in a hemorrhage of color
maple, aspen, gum at odds with each other
locust, sassafras, linden, oak
jockeying for place and the sun's privilege.
A million tongues and hands all ....
It is too much.

I need a controlled burn.
Retreat to the comfortable bias of line length
Retreat to the easy audism of rhythm
Remembering what first drew me here
Remembering again where it will all end.

Deciduous (1)

Early November:
sloshing about leaf fall at
Washington's Crossing.

Wind winnows words
squirrels scurry among
the silent oaks

shedding time
nature is sloughing
its excess

my mind
cleans itself too
air clear

thoughts
disappear
now

body

home

Ice Storm

The scent in the wind is sharp, clean
like the Buffalo winter of '76
after rain-glazed trees
were frozen with the temperature's drop
encasing every leaf, twig and branch in
a crystalline dream

we lay in the dark with our children listening
to icicles shattering with the sounds of bombs

a fairy world.

Who would have thought
that the falling of something so fragile
could create such explosions
sound waves
reverberating far into the future,
a hymn or an elegy perhaps
stowaway in the wind
as Thanksgiving approaches.

After Reading Roland Barthes' Camera Lucida

It is fitting that the photo is in black and white:
strolling barefoot down a summer sidewalk
me pushing the stroller
your hands in the air gesturing exuberantly
face caught in the moment's wonder
as I listen rapt to your words.

That day now a remote tale
from Arabian Nights,
a star that exploded long ago still here in the sky
light traveling these million years to let us know it was.
This photo in my hands, a creation of light, a testimony:
some genie caught us unaware in our joy
a gift to remind us, we did exist.

Deciduous (2)

Words desert me
like leaves from a sycamore
slowly, a brief hesitation
a hole where the petiole ends
and the search for a way to patch it.

Syllables pile around the trunk
discarded notes bereft of music.
Where will my mind be
when the wind blows through bare boughs?

I'd longed to be struck by lightning
sudden understanding
a rhapsody of autumn maples
sliced in between moment and moment
not this gradual deciduation
the leaf by leaf erasure to tabula rasa.

Zen in the Art…

The line arcs outward overhead
snapped back   released
snapped back   released
until it lands mid-center in the stream
runs
then slowly draws back again
completing the circle
in one liquid motion
before being cast again.
At any point a trout may bite
but it's not about the fish
which are always released
back into the water
it's about the focus
a way of centering self
to finally let go
so that fish, line, river,
man are all one
the way that breath is both
a cast in and out,
two parts of the same whole
a catch and release
of being.

Laurel Hill

We've chosen the place where we'll be buried
a hill above the Schuylkill.
The day is sunny and ripe for picnicking.
We imagine visitors
lounging among historic graves as the river
lazes its way below.
Perhaps they will bring wine
and—we hope—fried chicken.
Great-grandchildren will ask
whose names are on the plaque
in rocks on the side of the hill
and the parents will reply
"Once upon a time..."

Acknowledgments

Grateful acknowledgment is made to the editors and staff of the journals in which some of the poems in this book have been previously published.

Wordgathering, "Dan Simpson, Reading," "Math Instructor," "To Larry Eigner," "Cento: Lessening Light," and "Summa."
"*Schuylkill Valley Journal*, "Mom: San Francisco, 1943," and "MS."
Nine Mile "Homestead," "Palmyra Cove," and "Cento for David Simpson."
Lit Break Magazine. "Letter from Dubai" and "At a Café in Montreal."
One Art. "First Day of Winter," and "Second Drowning."
Connections "Laurel Hill."
Kaleidoscope. "Madison Pub."
Poetry Northwest "Little Litany."
Freefall. "Stuart in Heaven."
Referential "April."
Ariel XXIV "Seconds."
The Book of Donuts (J. Brown & S. Latham, Terrapin Books, 2017), "Donut Day at Inglis House."

"Madison Pub," "April," "Seconds," and "Dan Simpson, Reading" were all republished in a special edition of *Nine Mile.*
"Stuart in Heaven" was republished in *Wordgathering.*

Special thanks to poets Anne Kaier, Therése Halscheid, and Ed Northen, for their careful reading of the original manuscript and for the suggestions they provided. This book is dedicated to my wife Lora, my children Patrick, Maura, Melissa, Maya and Elijah, and my grandchildren Amelia, Connor, Jack, Andrew, Liam, Owen, Maggie, Daisie and Pasquale.

Prior to his retirement, **Michael Northen** was a teacher and educator for over forty years, teaching in a wide variety of circumstances including inner city, rural, and prisons, with elementary school students, learning disabled resource rooms, high school dropouts, women on public assistance and disabled adults. In all of these settings and populations, the use of poetry and the effort to get the work of students into publication was an important part of his teaching. From 1990-1992 he edited the *Chimera Poetry Magazine for Children,* a monthly magazine that cooperated with schools across the country to publish the work of young writers. At the 1992 Philadelphia Writers Conference his poetry won first place for both adult and children writing.

In 1997 he joined Inglis House in Philadelphia as the coordinator of education for GED and College degree programs and, at the urging of the residents there, began the Inglis House Poetry Workshop. All of its members, other than Northen were in wheelchairs and had multiple physical disabilities. At the time, there was almost no poetry available that reflected the experiences of the writers in the group. Throughout the next dozen years the group worked to change this situation by writing and discussing their own poetry and by soliciting the work of other disabled writers through annual poetry contests. The workshop published annual chapbooks of the winners and top poetry submissions. This work eventually resulted in the founding of the online journal *Wordgathering: A Journal of Disability and Literature*, with Northen as the editor-in-chief from 2007-2019.

During this time Northen completed his doctoral dissertation in education focusing on the use of disability literature in reading education. In 2011, together with poets Sheila Black and Jennifer Bartlett, he edited, *Beauty is a Verb: The New Poetry of Disability,* which won the American Library Award. In 2017 with Black and Annabelle Hayse, he edited an anthology of disability short fiction *The Right Way to be Crippled & Naked.* As this was going on he was also involved with planning and participating in panel discussions for the annual AWP meetings. He also joined with writer/ editor Sean Mahoney to establish the Disability Literature Consortium, which worked with disability literary magazines and writers to sell and help distribute their books.

In 2026 together with poets Camisha Jones, Travis Wing Chi Lau and Naomi Ortiz, Northen edited a second anthology of disability poetry *Every Place on the Map is Disabled: Poems and Essays*, published by Northwestern University Press.

Since retiring from *Wordgathering* in 2019 when it was turned over to Syracuse University, Michael Northen has returned to more personal writing, focused on family and personal meditation. Much of that writing is what makes up *The Only One in the Room with White Socks.*

www.ingramcontent.com/pod-product-compliance
Lightning Source LLC
LaVergne TN
LVHW090537110826
845146LV00003B/1136

* 9 7 9 8 8 9 9 9 0 5 1 2 4 *